THE PUG ADVENTURES

Ricky and Poe Travel to Italy

Written by Christina J Wood

Illustrated by Misha Malik

To all the children who want to be explorers someday—may you always ask questions about the world and appreciate its many cultures. Embrace the journey of discovery.

~Christina Wood

Copyright ©2025 Christina J Wood

Written by Christina J Wood
Illustrated by Misha Malik

Photo of Christina J Wood by Sherry Mount

Published by Miriam Laundry Publishing Company
miriamlaundry.com

All rights reserved. This book or any portion thereof may not be reproduced or used in any manner whatsoever without the express written permission from the author except for the use of brief quotations in a book review.

Saint Paul, Minnesota
Library of Congress Control Number: 2025904151

HC ISBN 978-1-77944-313-7
PB ISBN 978-1-77944-312-0
e-Book ISBN 978-1-77944-311-3

FIRST EDITION

"Pizza, spaghetti, lasagna, gelato...yes, I'd like to order all of those, please!" murmured Poe in his sleep.

"Wake up! Wake up! We're going to Italy today. Remember? We're going on vacation!" Ricky shouted, nudging his brother.

Poe jumped straight out of bed, his eyes sparkling with excitement.

In no time, the Pug brothers, Ricky and Poe, were packed and ready for their Italian adventure. Ricky was always looking out for his little brother, Poe, and made sure they had everything they needed for their trip to Italy.

They boarded the plane just in time! Up, up, up, and away they went, over the mountains and across the ocean.

During the plane ride, Ricky turned to Poe and said, "Don't forget the Golden Rule! Wave your yellow flag and use your pug mug to sniff out the best smells in Italy in case we get separated, okay?"

"Ubetcha!" shouted Poe, bouncing in his seat like a pogo stick. He was so excited, he almost wiggled right out of his seat belt.

When they arrived in Venice, the annual Carnival was in full swing.
The streets were crowded with dogs wearing sparkly costumes, munching on treats, and dancing to lively music.

"Let's go shopping for our costumes!" Ricky said, excited as ever.

They visited many shops, sniffing out the perfect outfits. Finally, they found their costumes! Poe picked out a long, red velvet cape—his favorite color—and a hat with big, furry red and orange feathers.

Ricky found a deep royal blue velvet cape and a fancy hat topped with a large blue feather.

"We look splendido!" Ricky exclaimed, striking a pose.

"Splendido!" Poe echoed, twirling his cape with a giggle.

They headed back to San Marco Square to eat pizza and dance with the other dogs.

Poe said, "This is the best sausage pizza in the whole wide world."

It was so good, their tails wagged with each cheesy, sausagey bite.

"Delizioso!" Ricky sang, licking his chops.

"Delizioso!" Poe shouted, his mouth full of pizza.

Then they both did a happy little pizza dance!

"Now let's get some gelato!" said Poe, jumping for joy.

"Ubetcha!" shouted Ricky.

The line stretched long and moved soooo slowly.
But finally, they reached the counter.

"Which flavor do you want?" Ricky asked, turning to Poe. But Poe was...

Gone!

Ricky's heart raced. Where did Poe go? He had disappeared.

He needed to find him, and fast. *Poe's the only brother I have AND we have a train to catch headed for Florence!* thought Ricky.

"Poe! Poe!" Ricky called, his voice carrying over the festival noise. He spun around, scanning the crowd of dancing dogs.

"Oh, no," he groaned. There were so many dogs wearing red capes and feathered hats—just like Poe! How would he ever find him?

Ricky remembered the Golden Rule—to wave his yellow flag if they ever got separated. So, he started to wave his yellow flag frantically in the air. "He'll never see me in all this chaos!" Ricky cried, his ears drooping in worry.

Just then, Ricky heard the big bells ringing in the church tower and looked up. *It's so tall, it's perfect! If I wave my flag from up there, Poe will definitely see me!* thought Ricky.

Without wasting another second, Ricky dashed toward the stairs and began climbing, huffing and puffing up four hundred steps!

Once he got to the top, he grabbed his yellow flag and began waving it wildly.
"Please see me, Poe, please...!" he cried.

"There he is!" screamed Ricky with joy.

Down below, he spotted Poe in a gondola, waving his yellow flag right back!

Ricky raced down the bell tower and Poe paddled the gondola closer.
But by the time Ricky got to the dock, Poe was gone.

"Oh, no! Now where did he go?" cried Ricky.

Just then, Ricky sniffed the air. Sweet, warm, buttery smells floated toward him. "Of course!" Ricky said, "The Golden Rule...follow your pug mug to the best smells! That's it—Poe must be following his pug mug to the bakery!"

Off he went, weaving through the crowd and calling, "Poe, Poe!"

Heart pounding, Ricky followed his nose through winding streets and over tiny bridges.

The sweet smell grew stronger with each step until—there! He saw a cozy bakery tucked between two buildings. When he pushed open the door, the little bell jingled and guess who spun around with a powdered frittella in his mouth?

You guessed it—Poe, with a nose full of powdered sugar, too!

"Ricky! You found me! I followed my pug mug like you said!" Poe exclaimed, waving his tail like crazy.

They hugged tightly. Ricky sighed with relief and said, "I'm so glad I found you and that you followed the Golden Rule! This would be no vacation without you, dear Poe. Now we must make a mad dash to catch our train to Florence, before it leaves without us."

"Wait!" said Poe, holding up a frittella. "You've got to try this! It's got raisins and a sweet filling, and you will LOOOOVE it!"

"Okay!" said Ricky.

The brothers enjoyed their delicious frittelle (with Poe on his second one) while Ricky's custard came squirting out all over the place!

With full tummies, they raced to meet the train.

With one last look at Venice's sparkling canals, the brothers boarded their train. "Florence, here we come!" Ricky cheered. As the train chugged through the rolling Tuscan hills, they snuggled in their seats with hot cappuccinos, moving ever closer to their next adventure.

When they arrived in Florence, it was raining cats and dogs!
The streets were slippery, and the rain was coming down so hard,
they couldn't even read the street signs.

"Where is the Uffizi Gallery?" Poe shouted, squinting through the raindrops.

"I think it's over here!" Ricky yelled back.

Suddenly, out of nowhere, a group of soggy, scruffy cats sprang from the shadows and chased after them.

"Run!" yelled Ricky, splashing through puddles. They ran through the pouring rain, splashing with each step in their new boots!

"Wait for me!" Poe yelled, as one sneaky cat grabbed the edge of his bright red cape, and then RIIIP! The cat tore a big hole right through it!

Just when it seemed like the cats might catch them, Ricky spotted something through the heavy rain. "There! The entrance!" he shouted.

"Quick, this way!" Ricky called, racing toward the Uffizi Gallery.
Poe ran after him, dripping wet, as they dashed inside—safe at last!

"We made it!" Ricky panted, shaking off the water.

"Look, Poe!" he said, pointing ahead.

There it was—the famous sculpture of Michelpuglio's Pug!
It was a towering, ten-foot marble masterpiece of a proud, regal Pug.

"Magnifico," Ricky murmured, his eyes sparkling.

"Magnifico," Poe whispered back, his tail wagging
as he gazed up at the incredible statue.

31

Room by room, each masterpiece told its own story. The sweet-faced *Cherub Pug Playing a Lute* seemed to play a melody just for them.

"Bellisimo!" they whispered in unison, their eyes wide with amazement.

Around the corner was *Surfer Pug*, the painting they had been waiting for—their favorite!

"I want to surf the waves just like *Surfer Pug*!" Poe shouted, staring at it in awe for several minutes.

Climbing the grand marble staircase to the next floor, they discovered the *Portrait of Chef Pug Giovanni.*

"Wow, splendido!" Poe exclaimed.

"Splendido, indeed!" Ricky said.

Then they spotted The Creation of Pugs painted by Michelpuglio.

"Bellissimo!" Ricky exclaimed, beaming from ear to ear.

"Bellissimo!" Poe echoed. "Do you think we could ever paint like that?" Poe asked.

"Let's find out! They have art classes on the second floor!" Ricky said.

Poe and Ricky put on their smocks and sat at their easels, ready for some fun. For inspiration, they decided to draw each other's portraits.

"Molto bene!" Poe said, admiring his work.

"Molto bene!" said Ricky, proudly looking at his masterpiece.

All too soon, it was time to head home—what an amazing adventure they had!

Once home, they proudly hung their portraits on the living room wall. "I am so glad we went on this trip together," said Poe, eating his frittella.

"So am I; it was such an adventure," agreed Ricky, sipping his cappuccino.

Admiring their paintings, Ricky smiled and said, "And now we'll always remember what a wonderful time we had."

Italian and English Words

ITALIAN		ENGLISH
Bellissimo	=	Beautiful
Cappuccino	=	Coffee
Delizioso	=	Delicious
Frittella	=	Donut
Frittelle	=	Donuts
Gelato	=	Ice cream
Gondola	=	Venetian Boat
Magnifico	=	Magnificent
Molto bene	=	Very good
Pizza	=	Pizza
Splendido	=	Splendid

Fun Facts of Venice

- Venice is called the "Floating City" because it was built on marshy land, and the buildings rise up right out of the water! Canals and bridges connect everything.

- The Venice Carnival has been around for a long time, since the Middle Ages! People gather at Saint Mark's Square to dance and wear fun costumes and masks.

- During the Venice Carnival, people eat yummy frittelle, which are like donuts, fried with raisins, orange peels, or lemon peels.

- St. Mark's Campanile is a huge bell tower at St. Mark's Basilica. It's the tallest building in Venice and was used by ships to find their way into the harbor.

Fun Facts of Florence

- Florence is the capital of Tuscany, a region in Italy.

- The train from Venice to Florence is super fast—it can go up to 190 miles per hour!

- The Uffizi Gallery is famous for its sculptures and paintings from the Renaissance period.

- Gelato, the yummy Italian ice cream, was first made in Florence in 1565!

- The *Statue of David* by Michelangelo stands tall at 17 feet in the Galleria dell'Accademia in Florence. It's made of marble and is one of the most famous sculptures in the world!

Testimonials

"The characters are charming and the author successfully highlights the endearing relationship between the two pug brothers. The storytelling is fun and lighthearted but also very educational. I thought it was an ingenious idea to incorporate information about Italian culture and geography in the storyline as a learning tool for children."
—Nancy Berry

· ·

"The story is engaging, captivating and educational. Children will easily fall in love with these two pug brothers through their exciting and colorful adventures. I look forward to reading the next book in the series."
—Reka Leopold

· ·

"Being an elementary teacher, your book brought so much happiness to my heart. I'm eager to share it with kids! I love the Italian words you taught us and they were so appropriate for the conversation! Ricky's tongue hanging out made me giggle! The message you sent to children is to follow through with a plan for safety. The costumes are so elegant that I wish I could touch them!"
—Leslie Erickson, St. Paul Elementary School Teacher, retired

About the Author

Christina Wood resides in Saint Paul, Minnesota, and draws inspiration for her stories from her two beloved pugs. Christina is committed to promoting cultural awareness and fostering an appreciation for diversity among young readers. With a passion for travel, she aims to share her experiences and knowledge with others. Through her engaging tales, she introduces children to a variety of cultures and traditions, encouraging them to embrace and celebrate the global tapestry of life.

Join Ricky and Poe as they embark on their adventures around the world!

www.thepugadventures.com

About the Illustrator

Misha Malik is a skilled graphic designer and children's book illustrator from Pakistan with over a decade of experience in the industry. With expertise in multiple illustration styles, Misha brings stories to life through 3D, 2D, digital, cartoon, whimsical, and watercolor techniques, among many others. Passionate about creating engaging and visually enchanting artwork, Misha strives to craft illustrations that inspire and delight young readers.

www.instagram.com/track_designs/

www.ingramcontent.com/pod-product-compliance
Lightning Source LLC
Chambersburg PA
CBHW041104070526
44583CB00002B/47